If My Mom Were a Platypus

This book was purchased with
grant funds from
The Community's Foundation

THE COMMUNITY'S FOUNDATION

If My Mom Were a Platypus

MAMMAL BABIES
AND THEIR MOTHERS

Dia L. Michels

ILLUSTRATED BY Andrew Barthelmes

Science, Naturally!®
Washington, DC

For Akaela, Zaydek, and Miralah—my mammal babies

Text and illustrations copyright © 2014, 2005, 2001 Dia L. Michels
Cover, Book Design, and All Illustrations by Andrew Barthelmes, Peekskill, NY

Paperback edition • April 2014 • ISBN 10: 1-9384921-1-0 • ISBN 13: 978-1-938492-11-2
E-book edition • April 2014 • ISBN 13: 978-1-938492-12-9 • ISBN 10: 1-9384921-2-9

Spanish paperback edition • June 2011 • ISBN 10: 0-9700106-8-0 • ISBN 13: 978-0-9700106-8-1
Dutch paperback edition • January 2012 • ISBN 10: 1-930775-46-6 • ISBN 13: 978-1-930775-46-6
    Published by Borstvoedingscentrum Panta Rhei, the Netherlands
Hebrew hardback edition • September 2010 • ISBN 10: 0-9678020-8-3 • ISBN 13: 978-0-9678020-8-4
    Published by Life Center, Israel

Originally published in English in 2001 (hardcover, ISBN: 1-930775-02-4), 2005 (paperback, ISBN: 1-930775-19-9) by Platypus Media, LLC

Published by:
    Science, Naturally!®
    725 8th Street, SE
    Washington, DC 20003
    202-465-4798 / Toll-free: 1-866-SCI-9876 (1-866-724-9876)
    Fax: 202-558-2132
    Info@ScienceNaturally.com / www.ScienceNaturally.com

Distributed to the book trade by:
    National Book Network
    301-459-3366 / Toll-free: 800-787-6859 / Fax: 301-429-5746
    CustServ@nbnbooks.com / www.nbnbooks.com

Library of Congress Cataloging-in-Publication Data

    Michels, Dia L.
    If my mom were a platypus : mammal babies and their mothers / Dia L. Michels ; illustrated by Andrew Barthelmes. -- Third edition.
        pages cm
    Includes index.
    ISBN 978-1-938492-11-2
    1. Mammals--Infancy--Juvenile literature. I. Barthelmes, Andrew. illustrator. II. Title.
    QL706.2.M53 2013
    599.13'92--dc23
                        2013044398

12 11 10 9 8 7 6 5 4 3

The content in all *Science, Naturally!* books correlates directly with the math and science standards laid out by the Center for Education at the National Academies. An articulation of the standards is available at ScienceNaturally.com. All *Science, Naturally!* books also align with the Common Core State Standards and the Next Generation Science Standards.

Teacher-written Activity Guide and Hands-On Demonstrations Guide to extend and expand the concepts in this book are available for free download at ScienceNaturally.com.

Schools, libraries, government and non-profit organizations can receive a bulk discount for quantity orders. Please contact us at the address above or email us at Info@ScienceNaturally.com.

Printed in the United States of America

EDITOR: Ellen E.M. Roberts, Where Books Begin, Bethlehem, PA
ASSOCIATE EDITOR: Ashley Parker, Washington, DC
RESEARCH DIRECTOR: Emily Schuster, Silver Spring, MD
RESEARCH ASSOCIATE: Judith Schaefer, Washington, DC
CREATIVE DIRECTOR: Douglas Wink, Inkway Graphics, Sante Fe, NM

Bridging the gap between
the blackboard and the blacktop

Contents

Many mammals are in danger of disappearing from our earth.
The symbol 🅴 indicates the animals whose existence is currently threatened.

If my mom were a platypus . . .

. . . I would have hatched from an egg!

How Were You Born?

To get ready for me, my mom built a nest beside a stream. In it she laid two leathery eggs the size of grapes. Platypus babies usually come in pairs. Our two eggs were stuck together so we wouldn't come apart or roll around. My mom scooped the eggs up with her tail and placed them on her belly. We rested there for ten days until hatching time.

I was bean-sized, bright pink, and hairless when I hatched with my eyes sealed shut. I clung to my mom's fur. Milk began to ooze out from the milk patches on her chest. I lapped the milk up from her fur.

How Did You Grow?

For nearly four months, I lived on my mom's milk. As I grew, my brown fur came in soft and silky. My eyes opened and I could crawl, growl like a puppy, and make kissing sounds. When my mom left the nest to get food for herself, she always plugged the entrance with mud so my twin and I would be safely hidden. Each time she returned she had to dig her way back into the nest.

What Do You Know?

When I was four months old, I left the nest for the first time. I was already over a foot (30 cm) long and weighed about one pound (454 g). My mom led me into the water for my first swim. She showed me how to catch insect eggs, which she crushed between two hard plates in her jaws for me to eat.

Now I am five months old. I still return to my nest to sleep with my mom. Very soon, though, I will leave to dig my own tunnel in another stream. There I will make a nest for my own babies someday.

8

And What Do You Eat?

I look on the bottom of the stream for food.
With my bill I find creatures to eat, like
shrimp and worms. My bill helps me find
food I can't see. It is soft and flexible, not
hard like a duck's bill. I curl my bill into a
flat tube that I use to suck in the shrimp
and worms. I keep them in my cheek
pouches until I get back up to the surface
of the stream. I grind my food in my jaws
while I float in the water.

9

Fascinating Fact

The male platypus is one of the few poisonous
mammals in nature. When another male gets too
close, the platypus stabs the offender with a spur
on his hind leg. Venom shoots out and stuns the
enemy, allowing the platypus to escape. Only the
male platypus has poisonous spurs.

If my mom were an African elephant . . .

. . . I would have been born with a big thump!

How Were You Born?

After nearly two years inside my mom, I was ready to be born. My mom moved close to another female elephant, steadying herself against the broad, warm back of this mom's helper. Then the other elephant cows and calves gathered round, rumbling loudly, waving their trunks, and flapping their ears. I dropped to the ground from between my mom's hind legs with a big thump.

Using their trunks, tusks, and front feet, my mom and the assisting elephant cleaned me up. Barely twenty minutes after I was born, I was standing on wobbly legs. My mom powdered me with huge clouds of dust to help dry me off. Then she slipped away for a drink. The other elephants took care of me until my mom came back.

How Did You Grow?

I was born big—about three feet (1 m) tall and over two hundred pounds (90 kg)—just the right size for a baby elephant. When my mom was standing or walking, I fit right underneath her. I let my trunk hang down limply to one side and reached up with my lips to a nipple between my mom's front legs. I nursed for a minute or two every half-hour. Sometimes I sucked my trunk just like a human baby sucking on his thumb.

Elephants grow up slowly. Until I am nine, I will spend at least half my time very close to my mom. A male elephant leaves his family group when he is between twelve and twenty years old. A female stays with the family her whole life.

What Do You Know?

My family teaches me things elephants need to know: how to recognize each other, how to find food and water, and how to swim using my trunk like a snorkel. As I learn, my mom takes good care of me. If I wander off, she comes after me. If I stumble, she wraps her trunk around my body and helps me to my feet. She helps me up hills and over fallen logs. She boosts me out of deep mud. She nudges and comforts me with her trunk. Sometimes, if I misbehave, she slaps me with it. My favorite thing is when she washes me with her trunk.

We always travel with our herd of other elephant cows and calves. My father and the other bull elephants usually only join us when it is time to mate.

And What Do You Eat?

My first teeth were only the size of quarters, not big enough to chew the tough leaves and grasses that elephants like. For the first three months of my life, my mom's milk was my only food.

I lost my baby teeth and grew larger new teeth so that I could eat plants. I will continue to nurse until I am over four years old and have tusks twelve inches (30 cm) long. By then, I will find all my own food. I will use my trunk to pick plants growing on the ground or high in the trees. I will spend sixteen hours a day looking for food.

Fascinating Fact

Elephant feet are tough enough for walking over rocks and stones, but they're also soft and spongy. Big, round feet help spread an elephant's weight over a large area. This takes the pressure of all that weight off the leg bones. With their big, soft, padded feet, elephants can move quietly, even though they can grow to weigh more than five tons (4.5 mt). Elephants barely leave footprints.

If my mom were a koala . . .

. . . I would have been born in a tree in Australia!

How Were You Born?

Before I was born, my mom already had a nest for me. Not a nest like a bird makes, but a soft, warm pouch on her belly. She sat in the branches of a eucalyptus tree and waited while I grew in her womb. The fur on her bottom was a fine, soft cushion. Finally, out I came—smaller than a grape! My eyes and ears were sealed shut. You could see my blood vessels through my thin skin.

I had tiny, needle-sharp claws on my front feet and strong shoulder muscles. I could crawl through my mom's thick fur to the small, round opening of her pouch. Her pouch opens backward, toward her feet, unlike a kangaroo's pouch. Once inside, I found two nipples. I latched on to one. It swelled so that I couldn't possibly fall off. I stayed there for six months drinking my mom's milk.

How Did You Grow?

Slowly, I began to grow as I drank my mom's milk. Her pouch stretched and grew with me. When my eyes finally opened, I peeped out for the first time. I was a scrawny little thing with short, flat, brown fur.

When I began leaving my mom's pouch for little outings, I smelled something good to eat nearby. I poked my head out and followed my nose. It led me to a soft, dark greenish substance, called pap, coming out of my mom's anus. It was made of leaves that my mom had chewed and swallowed.

As I began eating pap, my mom's milk became thicker and richer. Feeding on milk and pap, I grew fast. Within two weeks my teeth came in and I became the fluffy, furry koala that I am today.

What Do You Know?

By the time I was seven months old, I had outgrown the pouch and stopped breastfeeding. Now I curl up on my mom's lap to sleep. When I wake up I ride on her back as she moves from one clump of eucalyptus leaves to another.

By my first birthday my mom will be expecting a new joey. When he pokes his head out of her pouch, I will have to leave my mom. There won't be enough good leaves in her patch of trees to support all of us, so I'll have to go out and find a tree of my very own.

And What Do You Eat?

We koalas have a slow, lazy life. We sleep all day in our tree. Then at night we eat our favorite food—eucalyptus leaves. They contain plenty of water so I don't need to drink very much. I like eucalyptus leaves so much that I can stay in the same tree for days at a time. I eat box leaves and mistletoe, too.

Fascinating Fact

Eucalyptus is used to make cough drops—and because koalas eat so much eucalyptus, they smell like cough drops, too! The smell helps them keep fleas away. There are more than seven hundred kinds of eucalyptus trees in Australia, but koalas eat leaves from only fifteen of them. Their noses help them sniff out the right kind of eucalyptus leaves.

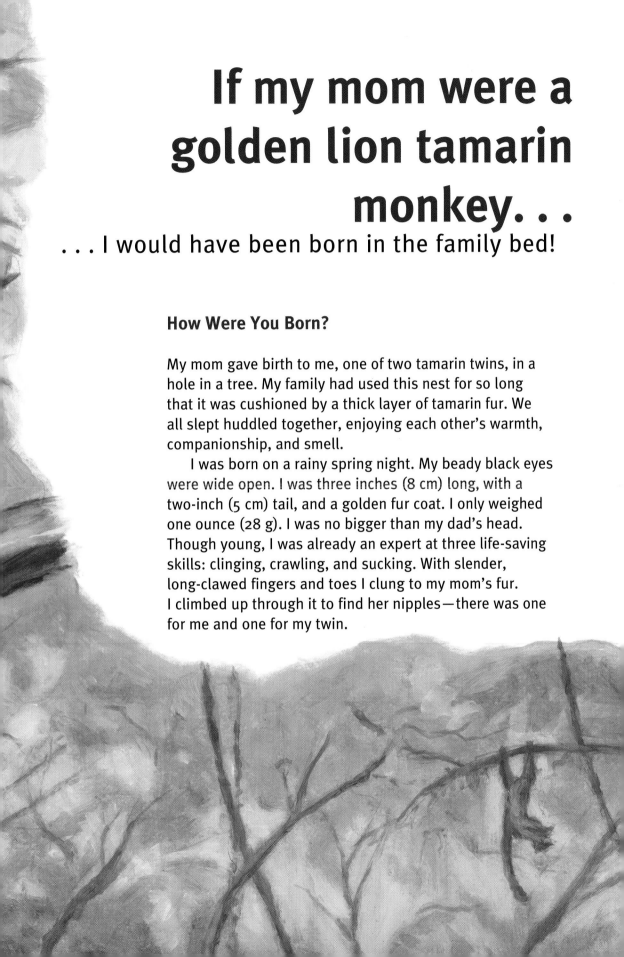

If my mom were a golden lion tamarin monkey...

... I would have been born in the family bed!

How Were You Born?

My mom gave birth to me, one of two tamarin twins, in a hole in a tree. My family had used this nest for so long that it was cushioned by a thick layer of tamarin fur. We all slept huddled together, enjoying each other's warmth, companionship, and smell.

I was born on a rainy spring night. My beady black eyes were wide open. I was three inches (8 cm) long, with a two-inch (5 cm) tail, and a golden fur coat. I only weighed one ounce (28 g). I was no bigger than my dad's head. Though young, I was already an expert at three life-saving skills: clinging, crawling, and sucking. With slender, long-clawed fingers and toes I clung to my mom's fur. I climbed up through it to find her nipples—there was one for me and one for my twin.

How Did You Grow?

For the first two weeks, I had to be carried all day long. My father and my older brothers and sisters all took turns carrying me. At first, I never left my mom's body unless I was snatched away. My instinct for clinging was strong, but sometimes one of the other monkeys in the nest would pull me off her back. My mom sometimes scraped me off against a branch, squeaking and nipping at me. She wasn't trying to hurt me. She could find food more easily without me.

By my third week, my mom was still feeding me, but my father was now carrying me most of the time. Two weeks later, I was big enough to start running, jumping, and climbing on my own. Soon my family didn't have to carry me anymore. I stopped breast-feeding, too.

20

What Do You Know?

My twin and I play a lot. We wrestle, grapple, pounce, and chase. Hide-and-seek is one of our favorite games. So is catapult: I lean on branches to bend them and they send me flying as they spring back into shape. Sometimes my twin and I both pounce on one of the adults. Usually our play is just fun, but if we make too much of a ruckus, an adult might punish the one who starts it.

And What Do You Eat?

Lion tamarin monkeys share their food. When I was five weeks old, I started eating solid food. Whoever was carrying me would pass back soft fruit or a juicy worm. Now that my first teeth have come in, I can enjoy crunchy grasshoppers and cockroaches, too.

I scamper about with the rest of my family as they eat and rest in our nesting hole. When I am a year-and-a-half old, I will leave home to start my own family.

Fascinating Fact

Tamarins may have two sets of twins a year. There are always infants around, so it takes the whole family to raise them. Not long after he stops nursing, a young tamarin will start to baby-sit for his younger brothers and sisters. If there's a choice, moms and sisters would rather carry female babies, and fathers and brothers would rather carry males.

If my mom were a Pacific gray whale . . .

. . . I would have been born underwater!

How Were You Born?

Before I was born, my mom spent the summer off the coast of Alaska, the most northwestern state in America. Big as a school bus and weighing thirty tons (27 mt), she ate nine hundred pounds (400 kg) of worms, crabs, and shrimp-like krill every day to get ready for a long trip south. There wouldn't be anything to eat along the way. The pad of blubber under my mom's skin would keep her—and me, still inside her—alive and warm.

Swimming slowly, my mom and other pregnant female whales spent about three months at sea. They traveled five thousand miles (8,000 km) to lagoons off the coast of Mexico. This journey is the longest-known migration of any mammal. Finally, my mom headed for the shallowest water, and I squirmed out, tail first, into the water. Three hours later, I could float by myself and swim a straight course.

How Did You Grow?

When I was born, I was about the size of a station wagon. Each day I drank about forty quarts (38 l) of my mom's milk to help me grow even bigger. In just two months, I weighed two tons (2 mt) and I was twenty feet (6 m) long. Unlike most mammals, whales nurse while moving. I swim with my mom as she glides through the water. The wave her body makes helps lift me up to her, so that I can nurse. All I have to do then is nudge one of two slits on her belly. Her milk comes out as thick as toothpaste, right into my mouth.

What Do You Know?

During my first two months, I stay close to my mom's side. If a killer whale approaches, my mom defends me. There are other moms and calves nearby, but my mom and I stay by ourselves.

The warm water is lovely, but we need food, so Mom and I begin the journey north. I am still nursing, so I'm not hungry yet. I have even grown my own pad of blubber. We will reach our Arctic feeding grounds in June. I will keep nursing for another couple of months. By that time, my mom will have given me six thousand quarts (about 57,000 l) of milk. I will be ready to start eating worms and crabs of my own.

And What Do You Eat?

Instead of teeth, gray whales have yellow bristles called baleen inside their mouths. The baleen works like a sieve. We swim along the ocean bottom, sucking up mud to get the small animals that live in it. We let the mud and water strain out, then we eat the worms and krill that remain.

Fascinating Fact

After their babies are born, most mammal moms lean down and break the umbilical cord with their teeth. Whales can't do that because they can't bend that far. Instead, they spin while giving birth, steering with their flippers. This spinning causes tension that helps the umbilical cord to snap.

If my mom were a giraffe . . .

. . . I would have been born into thin air!

How Were You Born?

When it was time for my birth, my mom headed away
from the other giraffes. She walked over to the place in
our home range where giraffes are born. It is called the
calving ground. I was born front feet first, with my little
head between my legs. I fell about five feet (1.5 m) from
my mom to the ground.

My mom licked me all over with her long, rough tongue,
paying special attention to my eyes, nose, and ears. My
short coat, already patterned with brown blotches, was soft
and woolly. My hooves were soft, but they hardened quickly.
Within the hour, I could stand on them. I began to suck on
one of my mom's four nipples. I was six feet (2 m) tall and
weighed one hundred and fifty pounds (68 kg) that first day.

How Did You Grow?

Many mammals spend their childhood
running, jumping, and playing, but giraffe
babies play less because we need to use our
energy to grow. I spent my days resting with other
calves my age. We touched and licked noses to get
to know each other. I ran around sometimes, but I spent
most of my first three months just lying or standing
around, scratching the ground, and licking my coat.

A giraffe protects herself by being big, so I needed to
grow as large as I could, as fast as I could. I grew over
three feet (1 m) in six months. Now I am nine feet (3 m) tall!

What Do You Know?

During the day, my mom goes away to eat. Thirteen feet (4 m) tall, with
large, sharp eyes, she can see for miles around. If danger threatens, she
will return quickly. She can kick predators with her long legs and hard,
sharp hooves. Usually I am safe because most giraffe predators, such as
lions, leopards, hyenas, and wild dogs, feed at night when my mom is
by my side. Giraffes band together in very loose herds. There are always
giraffes drifting in and out of my herd. Adult giraffes spend less than an
hour a day associating with each other and usually stay sixty feet (18 m)
apart. We are very quiet animals, but baby giraffes can bleat. Adults can
snort and roar.

And What Do You Eat?

Now that I am six months old, I have started following my mom as she feeds. She shows me how to strip the leaves off acacia trees with my long, flexible tongue.

Drinking water is hard—I have to bend my legs and then lower my neck to drink. It would be easy for a lion to attack me in this awkward position. Luckily, I can go for weeks without drinking because I get most of my water from leaves.

Toward the end of my first year, I will eat more leaves and nurse less. Just after my first birthday, I will stop nursing entirely. I will stay near my mom for another two months before beginning life on my own.

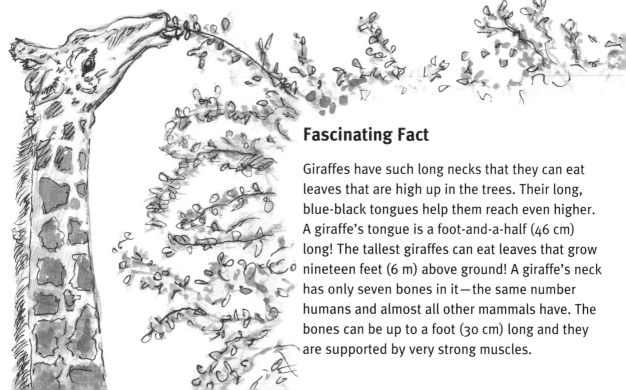

Fascinating Fact

Giraffes have such long necks that they can eat leaves that are high up in the trees. Their long, blue-black tongues help them reach even higher. A giraffe's tongue is a foot-and-a-half (46 cm) long! The tallest giraffes can eat leaves that grow nineteen feet (6 m) above ground! A giraffe's neck has only seven bones in it—the same number humans and almost all other mammals have. The bones can be up to a foot (30 cm) long and they are supported by very strong muscles.

If my mom were a least shrew . . .

. . . I would have been born to hustle!

How Were You Born?

Almost everything in a least shrew's life happens at top
speed. My mom scurried about with bits of dried grass,
leaves, and moss in her mouth to build a nest for me. With
her long, pointed snout, she wove the strands into a round
nest slightly smaller than a tennis ball, and she left little
openings for going in and out. She tumbled over and over,
shaping and hollowing it with her body.

When I was born I was the size of an almond and
weighed next to nothing. I was hairless and blind, with
blood vessels shining bright red through my thin skin and
little whiskers sticking out from my nose. On my tiny toes
were claws, perfect for climbing to a nipple to nurse. I was
one of seven babies. Bigger shrew babies push out the
smaller ones, who soon die—leaving their share of the milk
for the survivors.

How Did You Grow?

I grew up very quickly. By the end of two weeks I had grown fur and teeth. Two days later, my eyes opened. In another two days, I was almost the same size as my mom—who already had another batch of babies on the way. When I was three weeks old, I stopped nursing. I had to leave home, build my own nest, and find my own food.

What Do You Know?

I ran across a field to find a place for my nest. Owls, weasels, foxes, and snakes hunted for me, but I found a spot to burrow. In the spring I will have babies of my own. Like my mom, I will build a nest for them of grass and leaves. I will search for enough insects and worms to eat to keep myself alive and produce breastmilk for my babies.

And What Do You Eat?

Least shrews are so small and have so little body fat that they need to eat every two hours. Day and night, summer and winter, I run through burrows and grass tunnels, sniffing for food. I don't sleep at night: I eat around the clock and take naps between meals. I eat insects, centipedes, grubs, snails, earthworms, and even small frogs. If you put all the food I eat each day in one pile, it would be bigger than I am.

Shrews use their strong teeth more than most mammals. As we get older, our teeth get worn down from cracking snail shells and crunchy insects.

Fascinating Fact

Shrews are fierce fighters. Since they hunt for food all day and all night, they must defend their feeding grounds against other shrews. A shrew fight is something to see! Squealing and screaming, they lock on to one another and roll around, kicking and biting until one gives up. The loser takes off, with the winner nipping at her rump.

If my mom were a hooded seal . . .

. . . I would have been born on ice!

How Were You Born?

One dark day, my mom got out of the cold ocean. It was time for me to be born so she lay down on the ice. I appeared, still packed in a sack. I wriggled inside for a minute, broke out of the sack, and began moving around on the ice. Five minutes later, my mom rolled onto her side, and I began to nurse. When I wasn't nursing, my mom's nipples disappeared deep into her fur, close to her skin so nothing stuck out of her sleek body, which is so well-suited to swimming.

How Did You Grow?

I was three feet (1 m) long and forty-four pounds (20 kg) when I was born. I needed to gain weight fast, so my mom's body provided milk for me that was 60 percent fat—the richest milk of any mammal! I drank two gallons (8 l) of the rosy-beige milk every day. In just four days my weight doubled—I wasn't a baby anymore.

During that time, my mom had never left my side. She had fed and defended me against polar bears, male seals nearly twice her size, and even humans. Just four days after I was born, she slipped off the ice and returned to the sea. She had lost weight taking care of me and needed to gain it back quickly. Besides, she was already pregnant again and had to fatten up for next year's pup.

Now I am on my own.

What Do You Know?

After my mom left me, I didn't eat a thing for four weeks. I stayed by myself on the ice. In a month I lost more than a quarter of my weight. That's when I first tried going into the water. I swam around and caught fish to eat, just like I do now. I spend most of my time swimming in the sea. When I'm on land, I can't move very quickly, which makes me an easy target for predators. Seals only come to land or ice to mate or to give birth to their young. When seals are hurt or sick, they go onto land to rest.

And What Do You Eat?

Now that I can hunt on my own,
I eat fish like halibut, redfish,
and cod. I also eat shrimp,
clams, crabs, and squid.

When I dive, I close my nose
and throat so I won't swallow
the sea water. I swim to the
surface of the water with my
catch and eat it there. I don't
chew my food. I swallow it whole.

Fascinating Fact

Why would an animal that lives about thirty years spend only four days being a pup
and have the shortest nursing period of any mammal? Hooded seals live at sea,
but they give birth and nurse out of the water. The only surface
available is floating ice. Pups are born in the
spring when the ice is beginning to melt
and break up. A sudden storm might
send pieces crashing together,
crushing moms and pups. Or an ice
floe might split, and moms and
pups could be separated. A short
childhood helps avoid these perils.

If my mom were a Mexican free-tailed bat . . .

. . . I would have been one in a million (or more)!

How Were You Born?

I was one of millions of free-tailed bats born in a cave in Texas, in the southwestern part of the United States. Our moms left their winter homes in Mexico to gather together in that cave. Each bat had one baby.

I came out bottom first, with my wings folded around me. I was a big baby, already one-fourth the weight of my mom, but I was blind and nearly hairless. I had tiny sharp teeth, and my hind feet and thumbs were almost adult-sized.

My mom cradled me in her up-turned tail, nipped the umbilical cord, and licked me clean. Then I nursed while she gave me a thorough sniffing-over, squeaking constantly. I answered back in my high, clear voice. Although my mom would never recognize my face—bats aren't blind, but they don't see well—she learned my smell within thirty minutes. She also knows my voice so well that she can always pick me out from the millions of bat pups.

How Did You Grow?

My mom flew me to the nursery part of the cave. There I hung upside down, tightly packed with all the other pups. If you pulled at one of us, you would loosen a whole cluster of babies.

I grew rapidly. In just three weeks, I was almost adult-sized. In four weeks, I had grown soft, brown fur. By five weeks, my permanent teeth had come in and my wings spread nearly a foot (30 cm).

My mom came twice a day to nurse me for about twenty minutes each time. Unlike most mammals, she has nipples on the sides of her body, not on her chest. When she was ready to go, she would pull away from me. If I held on, she would drag me along until I let go.

What Do You Know?

Now that I am five weeks old, I can fly. Bats are the only mammals that can truly fly. At first I flew clumsily. Now I find my way using echolocation. I make squeaking sounds that echo off objects and tell me where those objects are. That way, I don't bump into anything.

A bat's wing is really a hand with sheets of skin stretched between the fingers. When I fly, I spread out my arms and fingers so the skin is stretched tight.

By moving my fingers, I can change the shape of my wings to steer. Free-tailed bats fly faster than most other bats.

And What Do You Eat?

Bats rest in caves during the day. At sundown, we leave to hunt for food. Mexican free-tailed bats eat moths, but nursing moms also eat flying ants to get extra nutrients they need to make milk for their babies.

As I began to fly, I learned to hunt, too. I caught few moths at first. Until I could catch what I needed to live, I survived on the fat that I stored while nursing. Now I can catch insects in my teeth, eating several thousand each night.

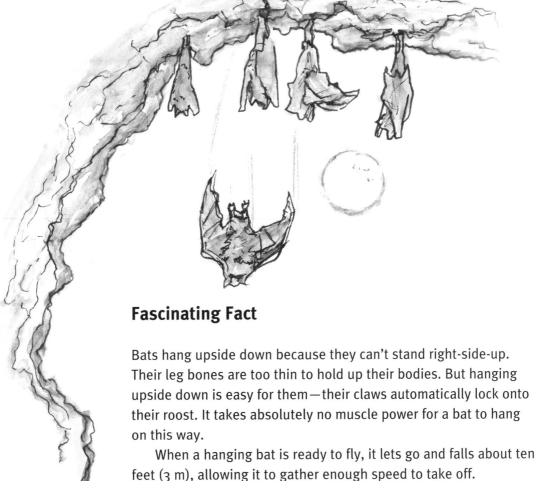

Fascinating Fact

Bats hang upside down because they can't stand right-side-up. Their leg bones are too thin to hold up their bodies. But hanging upside down is easy for them—their claws automatically lock onto their roost. It takes absolutely no muscle power for a bat to hang on this way.

When a hanging bat is ready to fly, it lets go and falls about ten feet (3 m), allowing it to gather enough speed to take off.

If my mom were a lion . . .

. . . I would have been born in hiding!

How Were You Born?

I was born in Africa in a place that was sheltered by rocks and tall grasses. My mom chose this spot to protect me from the leopards, eagles, hyenas, and enemy lions who would have liked to eat me. I was one of four lion cubs in the litter. When I was born, I was blind, toothless, and barely able to move. My only food was milk from my mom.

How Did You Grow?

When I was born, my mom carried me around by the scruff of my neck, even though some day I would grow to weigh four hundred pounds (180 kg)! For five weeks, I stayed in the den, safely hidden. Sometimes my mom left me for a whole day to go hunting for food.

When I learned to walk, my mom led me out of the hiding place. We joined the other lionesses—my mom's sisters and cousins—and their cubs. There are also a few adult male lions in our group, which is called a pride.

What Do You Know?

In our pride, the moms hunt and feed together. They defend their cubs and their territory. The biggest enemies are not other kinds of animals, but other lions. Male lions want to take over our pride, and females want to steal our feeding range. Lionesses live in groups to protect themselves from these other lions. Male lions help defend the pride, too, but soon enough they are driven off by other males. Lionesses are the main hunters and defenders of the pride.

And What Do You Eat?

Lions eat antelope, wildebeests, and buffalo. Adult males eat first, females eat next, and cubs eat last. Meanwhile, hyenas stand nearby, watching the feast and hoping to steal some dinner.

Slowly I am learning to hunt my own food. I practice stalking and pouncing. Lion cubs can spoil hunts by running ahead or meowing. I am learning to sit patiently and watch the hunting. My mom shows me how to kill, but doesn't help me do it.

It takes two years for my mom to teach me how to hunt. After they've learned my brothers and male cousins wander away from the pride, but we female cubs stay. One day I will go back to the den where I was born to give birth to my own cubs.

Fascinating Fact

Within a pride, lionesses help take care of each other's cubs, even when it comes to breastfeeding. A napping lioness who has been hunting all night doesn't pay much attention to who is suckling on her. Unlike most other mammal moms, who only nurse their own young, lionesses will make milk for any of the cubs in her pride.

If my mom were a polar bear . . .

. . . I would have been born in a snow cave!

How Were You Born?

Before I was born, my mom tunneled into a snow bank to hollow out a den for me. She made a hole in the top for air. She piled snow in front, so that warm air would stay inside. She crawled in, curled up, and dozed, waiting for my sister and me to be born.

    I was born with my short fur still wet. I had no fat on my body. My mom dried me off quickly and I snuggled deep into her fur to keep warm. I couldn't see or hear, but I could smell my mom's nipple. I crawled up her body and began to nurse.

How Did You Grow?

I was born the size of a guinea pig. My mom was four hundred times bigger than me!

I grew rapidly, drinking my mom's thick, creamy milk. At first, she lay on her side to feed me. As I grew, she sat against the cave wall and cradled me in her huge, furry arms. Sometimes she rocked gently, side to side. During this first month with her cubs, my mom didn't eat anything and never left the den.

At three weeks I could hear. Then my blue eyes opened so I could see. Two weeks later, I could chew and even walk a little. By four months, I weighed twenty-five pounds (11 kg). Sleek and fat, with a thick fur coat, I was ready to leave the den for the first time. Tagging along next to Mom, I explored the world by her side for the next two-and-a-half years.

48

What Do You Know?

Outside the den, I followed my mom, stepping in her big footprints. When I was tired or cold, I climbed onto her back. Soon after leaving the den, my mom led me into the water for my first swim. Polar bears float easily and are strong swimmers. We use our huge front paws to paddle and we steer with our hind legs. We can swim as far as sixty miles (100 km) a day in water so cold that most creatures would perish in it within minutes. We can even sleep at sea!

And What Do You Eat?

Polar bears eat seal meat. This is a messy business. My mom taught me to take a break from eating every twenty minutes and go to the water to wash off the grease and blood.

When I was a year old, I began to hunt my own seal meat. At first, I didn't catch anything. It takes two years to learn to catch a seal for food.

Now that I can hunt alone, I use my nose to track a seal for miles. I also listen for seals calling to each other underwater. Sometimes I grab a seal as he comes to the surface of the water to breathe. Other times, I find a seal resting out on the open ice. I move toward the seal by sliding across the ice on my belly, to take him by surprise.

Fascinating Fact

A polar bear looks white, but he isn't really. The long hairs in his shaggy coat are colorless and hollow. Sunlight bounces off them and makes them appear white. The sunlight flows into each hollow hair and carries heat to the polar bear's body. Beneath his hair, the polar bear's skin is black. That helps his body absorb heat. You can see the black skin on his nose, tongue, and the soles of his feet. When the sun isn't shining, the bear's blubber keeps him warm.

If my mom were a hippopotamus . . .

. . . I would have been born in a crocodile-infested river!

How Were You Born?

Before I was born, my mom found a quiet spot away from the hippo herd. She lay down in water up to her eyes and nose, and out I came—first my front feet, then my head, and then my hind feet. My cradle was the warm, brown water of a slow-moving river.

Immediately, my mom poked her big head into the water and boosted me to the surface to take my first breath. Then I went back underwater to nurse. I had to fold my ears down and close my nostrils to keep the water out. Twice every minute, I bobbed to the surface to breathe and swallow.

How Did You Grow?

My mom and I stayed away from the herd for two weeks, while I learned to float in the water by myself. For the first few days, my mom never left me, not even to eat. She nuzzled and scraped my skin gently with her teeth. She kept me safe from hungry crocodiles—she could bite them in two with her mighty jaws. If she had to move into deeper water, she would nudge me up onto her broad back to carry me.

Soon we rejoined the herd, and I continued to nurse and grow. By my first birthday, I was four times bigger than when I was born. I had stopped nursing and I had my full set of teeth. I will stay with my mom until I am five years old.

What Do You Know?

My herd spends the days in a pool in the river. Moms and calves, as well as a few males, crowd the water and the bank. Birds pick ticks from our backs. Because we are so big, we stick up out of the water. Turtles and even baby crocodiles climb aboard to lie in the sun.

During the day, I play and wrestle with other calves. Adults rest or court one another and mate. The males fight a lot—sometimes they throw water on each other, tusk-wrestle, or lunge and fall with a splash.

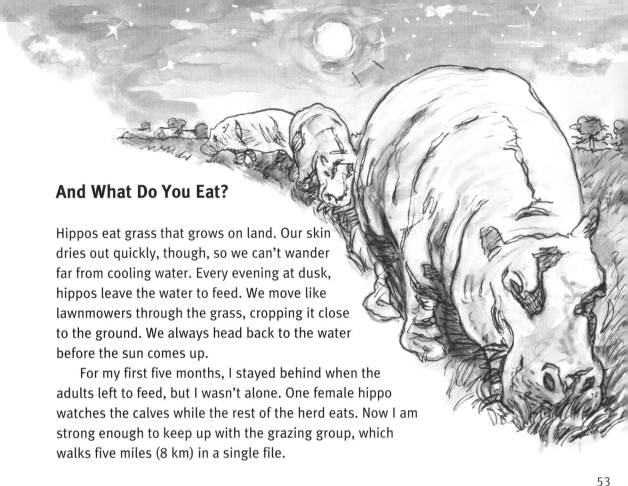

And What Do You Eat?

Hippos eat grass that grows on land. Our skin dries out quickly, though, so we can't wander far from cooling water. Every evening at dusk, hippos leave the water to feed. We move like lawnmowers through the grass, cropping it close to the ground. We always head back to the water before the sun comes up.

For my first five months, I stayed behind when the adults left to feed, but I wasn't alone. One female hippo watches the calves while the rest of the herd eats. Now I am strong enough to keep up with the grazing group, which walks five miles (8 km) in a single file.

Fascinating Fact

Hippos have a smelly way of sending messages to each other: they use their dung. If moms stand up to fight a big bull hippo who is threatening their calves, the bull will usually spray them all with dung. This tells the moms that he is backing off and they need not attack him. Males use this signal among themselves, too.

If my mom were an orangutan . . .

. . . I would have been born high and dry!

How Were You Born?

About three weeks before my birth, my mom began drinking lots of water from holes in trees. She also ate lots of termites to get the protein she needed. She had always built nests to rest in at night, but now she began building them during the day, too. One day, in the midst of a downpour, she made a quick nest seventy feet (20 m) above the ground. She gave birth to me. The nest kept us dry in the pouring rain.

I crawled into my mom's fur, holding on tightly. I looked like my mom, but with a pink face and a silky head with hair standing on end.

How Did You Grow?

For the next two days, my mom rested in her nest to regain her strength. Then she began to search for food. As she moved through the forest, I was always with her, clinging so tightly to the fur on her side or stomach that she didn't have to hold me. Like a bat, I was born knowing how to hang on.

I will continue to nurse, ride on her body, and sleep in her nest for more than six years. Young orangutans stay with their moms until the next infant arrives. Males begin to wander off then, but females often stay around for a while observing how babies are cared for.

What Do You Know?

I spend my days climbing, swinging, and yelling. I learn how to nurse upside down: I use a hand and a foot to hang from a branch right above my mom. Sometimes we stay with other adult females. If they have youngsters with them, I play with them. We might feed in the same tree for a day or so. Otherwise, we keep to ourselves.

Orangutans, unlike most apes, spend most of our time in trees, curving our fingers and toes like hooks over branches and vines.

And What Do You Eat?

All the while, I have been learning how to find fruit to eat. In a rain forest, fruit trees are widely scattered so keeping track of them is hard. I follow birds like hornbills and pigeons, who spot fruits from the sky as they fly. My favorite fruit is called a durian. It has prickles on its tough skin and sweet, stinky pulp inside. Orangutans also like to eat ants. Holding the back of my hand to a tree trunk, I let the ants climb over it. Then I put my hand in my mouth and nibble them off.

Fascinating Fact

It rains a lot in the forest where orangutans live, so they pick large leaves or big branches to use as umbrellas. They also cover their nests to keep them dry in the rain. Every single night, orangutans pull down leaves and branches to make a new place to sleep.

But my mom is a human . . .

. . . and I was born in a birthing center!

How Were You Born?

After I had been inside my mother's womb for nine months, she began to have contractions, which meant that I was ready to be born. My mom and dad went to the birthing center, where the midwife was waiting for us.

Several hours after we arrived, my mom felt it was time for me to come out. With my dad at her side, she gave a few mighty pushes. The midwife guided my head so my shoulders and body could slide out. Then she placed me on my mom's warm belly. I took my first breath of air and gave a cry. I heard my dad say my name. He cut the umbilical cord that had provided nourishment to me in the womb. From now on, I would have to breathe with my lungs and eat through my mouth. I heard my mom's familiar voice as she lifted me to her breast. I snuggled right in and began to suckle.

How Did You Grow?

My mom's breastmilk gave me everything I needed to grow big and strong and healthy. She let me nurse whenever I was hungry. By the time I was two weeks old, I was drinking nearly a quart (1 l) of milk a day.

I grew slowly, compared to most other mammals. After a month, I began to smile and laugh. In the next few months, I learned to hold up my big heavy head and, later, to roll over. At six months, I sat all by myself for the first time. By nine months, I could crawl and, by my first birthday, I had learned to walk a little.

By the time I was a few years old, I lost interest in nursing, but I still wasn't ready to take care of myself. Most baby mammals leave their moms and become adults soon after they stop nursing, but human children need their parents to watch over them long afterward.

What Do You Know?

As I grew up, I learned about all kinds of things: how to find food, how to talk, and how to walk. Humans have large brains. They also have hands that can do many different things, like pitching a ball, changing a channel, or picking up a pin. Since humans have to learn many things in order to survive, human babies usually stay with their parents for about twenty years.

Humans walk on just two feet, so our hands are free to do lots of things. When I was three months old, I started to use my hands to hit at things, and three months later, I could reach for things and grab them. Now I can use my hands to paint a picture, put a puzzle together, or build a birdhouse.

And What Do You Eat?

At about six months, I started eating little spoonfuls of soft food, but my mom's milk was still my main meal. My teeth began to grow one after another. I had my first full set of teeth at two-and-a-half, so I could eat the same food as my parents, but first they cut it into very small pieces for me.

Unlike other mammals, humans cook their food. Cooking kills germs and softens tough fibers so that humans can eat a greater variety of foods than any other mammal.

Fascinating Fact

A baby grows inside her mom's uterus, or womb. The baby is connected by the umbilical cord to the placenta, an organ attached to the lining of the uterus. The placenta gives the baby the oxygen and food she needs while she grows inside her mom. Once the baby comes out of the mom, the placenta comes out too. Then the connecting umbilical cord is no longer needed, so it is cut off. It leaves a stump that falls off after a few weeks. What's left is called the belly button.

GLOSSARY

anus – The opening through which solid waste (poop) leaves the body.

baleen – The plates that hang from the upper jaws of whales which are used as a sieve to strain food from mud and water.

birthing center – A place designed to look and feel like a home that provides care for mothers before, during, and after the birth of their babies.

blubber – The layer of fat below the skin of whales and other marine animals.

bull – The name for an adult male of certain large animals such as a cow, alligator, elephant, hippopotamus, or moose.

burrow – To dig a hole in the ground that will be used to hide or live in.

calf – The young of certain large mammals such as an elephant, whale, cow, giraffe, or hippopotamus.

calving ground – The site where certain large mammals give birth.

child – A human being between birth and puberty.

contraction – The rhythmic tightening of the uterus which helps push the baby out of the mother's body during birth.

crustacean – An aquatic arthropod that has a segmented body with a hard outer shell such as a lobster, crab, krill, or barnacle.

cub – The young of certain meat-eating animals such as a bear, wolf, or lion.

dung – The solid waste of an animal; poop.

durian – The fruit of a tree that grows in Southeast Asia. It has a hard, prickly rind and soft pulp.

echolocation – A system which bats and some other animals use to find their way around. They make high-pitched noises that echo off objects and return to their ears, telling them where those objects are.

eucalyptus – A tall tree, native to Australia, known for its strong-smelling leaves.

flipper – A wide, flat limb adapted for swimming that is seen in aquatic animals such as a platypus, seal, whale, or sea turtle.

ice floe – A large, flat sheet of floating ice.

infant – A baby in the earliest period of life.

joey – A baby marsupial such as a kangaroo or a koala.

krill – A small marine crustacean (aquatic animal that has jointed legs and a hard outer shell). Krill are the main food of baleen whales.

lagoon – A shallow body of water separated from the sea by low sandy dunes.

mammal – A warm-blooded animal that has a backbone, hair or fur, and makes milk to feed its babies.

midwife – A person who helps mothers give birth.

migration – The process of periodically moving from one area or climate to another. Some whales, birds, and fish migrate.

nursing – To feed at the breast; to suckle; to breastfeed.

nutrient – A source of nourishment, especially in food.

pap – A soft, dark greenish substance made of leaves that a mother koala chews and swallows. It then leaves her body through her anus and is eaten by her baby.

placenta – An organ in most mammal mothers formed in the lining of the uterus. It provides nutrients and oxygen to the unborn baby through the umbilical cord and also receives the baby's waste. *See also* **uterus.**

predator – An animal that hunts and eats other animals.

pregnant – Used to describe a female mammal who is carrying a developing baby within the body.

pride – A group of lions.

primate – Any member of the subcategory of mammals comprising apes, monkeys, and humans. Chimpanzees, gorillas, gibbons, lemurs, and orangutans are all primates.

pup – The young of certain animals such as a dog, wolf, fox, bat, or seal.

suckle – To nurse or breastfeed; *see also* **nursing.**

tension – The state of being stretched tight.

umbilical cord – The flexible cord that connects a developing unborn baby with the placenta in his mother's uterus, or womb. The umbilical cord carries oxygen and nutrients to the baby and removes his waste. *See also* **nutrient, placenta, uterus.**

uterus – In most mammals, the organ in which the baby develops before birth; the womb.

venom – The poisonous liquid that some animals put into their victims' bodies by biting, stinging, etc. Spiders, snakes, and platypuses all have venom.

womb – In most mammals, the organ in which the baby develops before birth; the uterus.

INDEX